C000148225

the little book of
US

Hardie Grant

QUADRILLE

"It takes two flints to make a fire."

LOUISA MAY ALCOTT

Us = you and me

Us = unique

Us = precious

Us = eternal

Two letters that mean so much, reveal so much and can never be repeated, because we are US.

*"I was born when you kissed me.
I died when you left me.
I lived a few weeks while you loved me."*

HUMPHREY BOGART
As Dixon Steele in a Lonely Place (1950)

Definition of 'us'

Used by a speaker to refer to himself or herself and one or more other people as the object of a verb or preposition. Can also be used in an informal way to refer to oneself.

Originates from Old English *ūs*; akin to Old High German *uns* (us), Latin *nos*.

*"Alone we can do so little;
together we can do so much."*

HELEN KELLER

"Let us always meet each other with a smile, for the smile is the beginning of love."

MOTHER TERESA

Us

What is there about that word
which changes everything?
Perceptions crumble in the mind;
assumptions all take wing.
I was alone, and I was 'me',
I had so much to do.
The world was vast, my choices huge,
Then one day, I met you.

My mind encompasses the 'you';
changes from 'then' to 'now'.
'We' are the person who decides
what I knew anyhow.
How strong the state of 'us' becomes:
it changes how we see.
The landscape moves and takes me far
from how 'I' used to be.

VIV APPLE

"We are one, after all, you and I. Together we suffer, together exist, and forever will recreate each other."

PIERRE TEILHARD DE CHARDIN

Two souls that come together to make something new: a shared vision of the future. Working as a team, we weave memories that create the tapestry of us. Unspoken, yet set in stone, our union is a piece of magic.

"If we do not hang together, we shall surely hang separately."

BENJAMIN FRANKLIN

Us means belonging, being part
of something with someone else.

"Individually, we are one drop. Together, we are an ocean."

RYUNOSUKE SATORO

In 'us' there is power and potential, whispers of things that will eventually be given voice. Together we are strong.

According to folklore, humans weren't created to live alone. We were formed as perfect pairs, male and female: twin halves in tune and in love, together for eternity. But, as with all things, the winds of change passed through, and like a hurricane ripped the two souls apart. Each individual was flung to the other side of the earth, disconnected, isolated and bereft. From this moment on, humans craved company, and yearned for the connection they'd once cherished so lovingly. This goes some way towards explaining our constant search for the one who will make us feel whole again.

Us can be two, three or more people. Whether a collective or a couple, lovers or friends, 'us' is about connection.

A sense of us

Check in with each other from time to time and be mindful of how the other person is feeling. Get a sense of where you are in the relationship and where you're going. Most importantly, communicate, for it is through communication that 'us' really comes alive.

"Love does not consist in gazing at each other, but in looking outward together in the same direction."

ANTOINE DE SAINT-EXUPÉRY

First there was me, and you, two people destined to meet. Then there was us, the thing we've become – that special space between us and the love we share.

"An invisible red thread connects those destined to meet, regardless of time, place or circumstances. The thread may stretch or tangle, but never break."

ANCIENT CHINESE PROVERB

Red thread of Destiny

According to Chinese legend, the Red Thread of Destiny, also known as the Red Thread, or String of Fate, is an invisible cord that binds us together – 'us' being two people who are destined to meet. The gods, in their magnificence, decided to tie invisible red threads around the ankles of future lovers, in the hope that they would find their way to each other and eventually marry. Another version of soulmates, these individuals would feel a gentle tug and find themselves pulled ever closer.

Yue Xia Lao is the lunar god responsible for this matchmaking, which is no surprise since he's also associated with marriage and commitment. The Red Thread of Destiny also makes an appearance in an ancient Chinese parable, but in this tale it is the 'old man in the moonlight' who ties threads around the ankles of future couples.

For us

Invest in some red thread, yarn or string, and make two bracelets: one for you and one for your other half. Get creative and thread on some red beads or leave as a simple tie to represent the bond you share.

If your 'us' is feeling shaky and you'd like to strengthen the ties between you, write down all the things that make you 'us' – the things you appreciate about your partner, the things that make you smile. Open your heart and let the words flow. Roll up the paper into a scroll and pop a photograph of the pair of you together inside, then tie securely with some red thread or string. Keep in a safe place as a love token to cement your bond.

The ties that bind don't have to be physical. Every time we meet someone, we forge a bond, a spiritual cord that ties us together. Depending on the relationship we have with this person, it can be light as a feather or sturdy as steel. It can be loose and flexible, keeping us connected over long distances, or short and rigid with little room to move. Consider your most important relationships and how they make you feel. Are you happy with the tie that binds, or would you like to change it?

Symbols of us

In folklore, symbols were often used to represent togetherness and to balance masculine and feminine energy. These symbols were used in rituals by the ancients to forge sacred unions and foster harmony.

Yin and yang

The Chinese symbol of balance brings together two elements, one black and one white, which interlock in a circle to represent male and female energy. Slotting together with ease to create a sense of equilibrium and strength, yin is female and yang is male; each contains a seed of the other within them.

Take inspiration from the yin yang symbol, and use it as a way to share time, tasks and precious moments. Draw a circle on a piece of paper and split it in two, like the symbol. Take half each and write things you'd like to do or share with your partner, then make a point of choosing one from each to complete every week.

Awen

This Celtic symbol has two outer rays – one male and one female. The third, central ray shows the balance and power maintained between them. In each case, the union of masculine and feminine energy brings something new, the potential for great things, happiness and a sense of balance. The twin spiral, also Celtic, is another symbol of equilibrium and is often likened to the yin yang symbol.

The three parallel rays of the awen symbol represent two people, who then create a third ray, the light between them. What is the light between you and your partner? What do you create together? If you're not sure, ask friends and family how they see you as a partnership. Consider what you'd like to create as a couple, and how you complement each other.

For us

Incorporate symbols of 'us' in your home décor, to re-enforce the special relationship you share and to remind you to spend quality time together.

"In the confusion we stay with each other, happy to be together, speaking without uttering a single word."

WALT WHITMAN

There's no set formula to meeting 'the one'. Whether you're into online dating, or prefer to meet socially or through work, you can never tell when it will happen. Where does the spark come from? Is it some divine blessing, or something we carry within us, which only that special someone can ignite? And once the flame is burning, how do we keep it from wavering? It is this sense of the unknown, the timeless mystery of the human heart, that makes each relationship a thing of wonder.

"Love is our true destiny. We do not find the meaning of life by ourselves alone – we find it with another."

FR. THOMAS MERTON

According to a 2018 survey by the UK's National Rail, most Brits meet their future wife or husband at social events, rather than through work or actively looking for dates online. Of the 2,000 questioned, most claimed that they met their soulmates on days or evenings out with friends. One in ten married a childhood sweetheart, while one in five met at work.

"When you fish for love, bait with your heart, not your brain."

MARK TWAIN

Ten places to find romance

1. At school

2. At work

3. On public transport

4. At the gym, or anywhere else you work out

5. Walking the dog

6. At a party

7. In a waiting room

8. Shopping

9. Grabbing morning coffee

10. At a wedding

"No one can live without relationship. You may withdraw into the mountains, become a monk, a sannyasi, wander off into the desert by yourself, but you are related. You cannot escape from that absolute fact. You cannot exist in isolation."

JIDDU KRISHNAMURTI

Relationship slang

Chatting up

Asking out

Dating

Courting

Stepping out

Hooking up

Going out

Seeing someone

Going steady

Being exclusive

Loved up

Getting engaged

Getting hitched

Put a ring on it

Tying the knot

Hanging out

Netflix and chill

Getting it on

Main squeeze

Partners in crime

My type on paper

Crack on

Shacked up

Courtship

In 1590s, the term 'courtship' meant "the wooing of a woman, attention paid by a man to a woman with the intention of winning her affection and ultimately her consent to marriage".

By the 1830s, the term was used to describe a period during which a couple mutually develops a romantic relationship with a view to marriage.

"I want to hear you think.
I want to see your thoughts."

ABIGAIL ADAMS

"How did it happen that their lips came together? How does it happen that birds sing, that snow melts, that the rose unfolds, that the dawn whitens behind the stark shapes of trees on the quivering summit of the hill? A kiss, and all was said."

VICTOR HUGO
Les Misérables

How did we first begin? Was it a momentary glance that caught my attention, the sparkle in your eye that played with my heartstrings? How did you woo me so? And how now, do I forget these things, that were once as crucial as the air I breathe?

"Romance is everything."

GERTRUDE STEIN

Speak kindly to each other. Choose your words well, for words have power and substance. They can lift the heart to the heavens, or slice through it without drawing a drop of blood.

Ten romantic ways to say I love you

You complete me.

You are the sunshine that lights every day.

I can't imagine a world without you in it.

You're my lobster.

I want to spend my life with you.

My heart aches for you when we're apart.

You are my universe.

Your name is etched on my heart.

Nothing in this world compares to you.

You are my everything.

"For there are moments in life,
when the heart is so full of emotion,
That if by chance it be shaken,
or into its depths like a pebble
Drops some careless word,
it overflows, and its secret,
Spilt on the ground like water,
can never be gathered together."

HENRY WADSWORTH LONGFELLOW

Since the beginning of time, mankind has captured heartfelt sentiment by putting pen to paper. These outpourings of emotion, known as 'love letters', found favour in the mid-eighteenth century, but the first published love note emerged in the early twelfth century between Peter Abelard, a leading French philosopher, and his student, Héloïse. Being both beautiful and 22 years younger than Abelard, she was also the niece of Canon Fulbert of Paris. Héloïse soon fell pregnant as a result of their passionate affair. To escape her uncle's wrath, she withdrew to a convent outside of Paris.

Abelard fared worse, being castrated by the Canon's kinsmen. While this could have been the end to their romance, they continued to write to each other, sharing innermost thoughts and feelings in a bid to bridge the divide between them.

From a love letter written by Oscar Wilde to Lord Alfred Douglas

"Everyone is furious with me for going back to you, but they don't understand us. I feel that it is only with you that I can do anything at all. Do remake my ruined life for me, and then our friendship and love will have a different meaning to the world. I wish that when we met at Rouen we had not parted at all. There are such wide abysses now of space and land between us. But we love each other."

Sometimes the strength of 'us' can change society completely.

Oscar Wilde's affair with Lord Alfred Douglas and Wilde's later imprisonment for homosexuality in 1895, scandalised Victorian Britain. However, the poignancy and tragedy of their relationship marked the beginning of demands for gay rights and recognition.

Love songs

(Everything I Do) I Do It for You
Bryan Adams

My Heart Will Go On
Céline Dion

I Will Always Love You
Whitney Housten

Can't Help Falling in Love
Elvis Presley

I Don't Want to Miss a Thing
Aerosmith

I Swear
All-4-One

True Colours
Cyndi Lauper

Chasing Cars
Snow Patrol

When You Say Nothing at All
Ronan Keating

Wonderful Tonight
Eric Clapton

All of Me
John Legend

Eternal Flame
The Bangles

Make You Feel My Love
Adele

"*Caresses, expressions of one sort or another, are necessary to the life of the affections as leaves are to the life of a tree. If they are wholly restrained, love will die at the roots.*"

NATHANIEL HAWTHORNE
The American Notebooks

A relationship must be tended daily. It must be fed and watered with love and attention and kept free from the weeds of jealousy. As it grows, it still needs the same amount of care as if it were a tiny sapling. Don't let it go to seed, or wilt away to nothing. Remember how you nurtured it in the first flush of spring, and how it flourished from your careful touch.

"You don't have to be singing about love all the time in order to give love to the people. You don't have to keep flashing those words all the time."

JIMI HENDRIX

Romance doesn't have to be extravagant. A cup of tea made with love and served with a smile warms the heart more than fancy jewels or poetic ministrations.

> *"Breathless, we flung us on
> a windy hill,
> Laughed in the sun,
> and kissed the lovely grass."*

RUPERT BROOKE
The Hill

A casual stroll through the park can set your heart fluttering if both partners are in the moment, fully present and engaged with each other and their surroundings.

Surprise your loved one with a picnic full of favourite treats. Find a spot you like out in the countryside and enjoy the view and each other's company.

*"How far away the stars seem,
and how far
Is our first kiss, and ah,
how old my heart!"*

WILLIAM BUTLER YEATS
Ephemera

Recreate your first date and relive those feelings of exhilaration. Whether it's a visit to the cinema, a drink or time spent idly chatting, pretend you're doing it all over again and enjoy the moment.

Dress up for dinner and serve your partner his or her favourite meal by candlelight.

Create a memory box and fill it with mementos from your relationship. Add to it regularly to keep the flow of love alive and take joy in the memories of each memento you treasure.

"Two lovers in the rain have no need of an umbrella."

JAPANESE PROVERB

"The hours I spend with you I look upon as sort of a perfumed garden, a dim twilight, and a fountain singing to it. You and you alone make me feel that I am alive. Other men it is said have seen angels, but I have seen thee and thou art enough."

JAPANESE PROVERB

Romantic customs around the world

Romance is taken seriously in Romania. They have their own version of Valentine's Day known as *Dragobete*. Named after the pagan god of love, this day is all about the chase. It starts with the ladies gathering in the woods to collect flowers. They are swiftly followed by the gentlemen, who pursue them in a chase home. Any lucky lady caught receives a kiss, and this is considered an informal engagement by the entire village.

In the village of Sonkarjavi in Finland, they embrace the spirit of teamwork with a yearly 'wife carrying' competition. The champion wins his partner's weight in beer.

Being pelted by an apple in ancient Greece meant you were the apple of someone's eye! Akin to a marriage proposal, the apple was associated with Aphrodite, goddess of love.

Verona's Casa di Giulietta, is a fourteenth-century house believed to have belonged to the Capulets. It's also a hotspot for love, being associated with one of Shakespeare's most romantic plays, *Romeo and Juliet*, and has thousands of visitors every year. Those looking for romance write handwritten notes and place them in the wall beneath the balcony. There's also a statue of Juliet, which is said to bring good fortune in love to those who rub her right breast.

In the small village of Miao, which lies in southwest China, men serenade women in a bid to win their hearts. In return, the ladies cook them rice, which is dyed different colours and parcelled into a handkerchief. Inside this bundle of love, there's a secret message which reveals how each lady feels about her prospective beau. Two chopsticks and her heart is yours; one means she is undecided. And if she has added garlic, then it's a definite refusal.

On St Dwynwen's Day, which falls on 25th January, Welsh men give the object of their affections a wooden spoon which they've lovingly hand-carved. If the spoon is returned, the feeling isn't mutual.

Salty bread is the cure for singledom in Armenia. Those looking for love should fast for the entire day before St Sarkis Day, then munch on salty bread. The snack must be made by a happily attached or married woman. It's thought that the bread conjures dreams of your future love, and, being salty, makes the dreamer thirsty. If the potential soulmate offers water in the dream to quench this thirst, a note must be made of how clean it is. If it's clear and fresh, then the marriage will be happy and blessed, but muddy water denotes unfaithfulness in the union.

Put pen to paper and compose a poem to a friend or loved one. Take your time and choose your words carefully to convey what that person means to you.

*"Two such as you with such a
    master speed
Cannot be parted nor be swept away
From one another once you are agreed
That life is only life forevermore
Together wing to wing and oar to oar."*

ROBERT FROST
The Master Speed

When we fall in love, we see the potential for goodness in another person. As philosopher Irving Singer claimed, we recreate the person; using our imagination we see them in a new light, giving value to their very existence.

There is no such thing as perfect,
only perfect for you.

Our foibles and faults are what make us unique. If you can accept this in another person, then they could be the right one for you.

"*It is not our purpose to become each other; it is to recognize each other, to learn to see the other and honour him for what he is: each the other's opposite and complement.*"

HERMANN HESSE
Narziß und Goldmund
(Narcissus and Goldmund)

Give-and-take works every time.
We all make mistakes, and we all
need forgiveness.

Say sorry and mean it.

Accept apologies and mean it.

"Once a woman has forgiven her man, she must not reheat his sins for breakfast."

MARLENE DIETRICH

Remember the things that brought you together: the likes, loves and interests. Go back to these things and make time for them, and you'll rediscover the first flush of romance.

Treat your relationship like a fine work of art. Give it light and space enough for the colours to blossom.

You do not need to live in each other's pockets; outside interests and friends add flavour and interest to a relationship.

" But let there be spaces in your togetherness and let the winds of the heavens dance between you. Love one another but make not a bond of love: let it rather be a moving sea between the shores of your souls."

KHALIL GIBRAN
The Prophet

"*Absences are a good influence in love and keep it bright and delicate.*"

ROBERT LOUIS STEVENSON
Virginibus Puerisque

Laugh together often. Laughter is the glue to romance, the best medicine for an ailing heart, and a sure-fire way to ignite the flames of passion.

Find the humour in every day and remember to share the laughs with the one you love.

Learn to laugh at yourself; you'll see the positive in any situation, while helping you maintain a relaxed and joyful countenance.

*"May this marriage be full of laughter,
Our every day a day in paradise."*

RUMI
The Marriage

Karam and Kartari Chand, who lived in England after marrying in India in 1925, are reported to be the longest married couple in the world. They were together for 90 years and 291 days. Karam died in 2016 at 110, and they left eight children and 27 grandchildren.

"There is no more lovely, friendly and charming relationship, communion or company than a good marriage."

MARTIN LUTHER

Whether you believe in marriage or prefer to do things in a more informal way, it's natural to want to make a commitment to your other half. This stems back to ancient times when men and women came together to form a sacred union. The commitment made, whether verbal, official or through some kind of bonding ritual, helps to cement the relationship. Like an anchor, it provides strength and stability, and something to draw upon when the going gets tough.

The UK's Office for National Statistics reports a decline in marriages, according to the most recent available figures. While there were 239,020 weddings in England and Wales in 2015, there were significantly more in 2014, when 247,372 couples tied the knot. This is a decrease of 3.4 per cent. The rising cost of weddings, along with lower social expectations and couples prioritising education and getting on the property ladder before getting hitched, appear to be the main reasons for the drop.

According to statistics from 2015, the average age a woman gets married in England and Wales, is 35.1 – up from 34.6 the previous year. The average age for men is 38, up a year from 2014.

Leap year

According to an old Irish legend, St. Brigid of Kildare made a deal with St. Patrick to allow women to pop the question to their male suitors who were too shy to ask. At first he granted women the permission, but only once every seven years, but at Brigid's insistence, he relented and allowed proposals every leap day. The tale then suggests that Brigid immediately dropped to her knee and asked Patrick to marry her, sadly he refused, kissing her on the cheek and offering a silk gown to soften the blow.

Leap year customs

Grecians consider marriage during a leap year to be inauspicious, and the relationship is thought likely to end in divorce.

Finnish women are advised to propose only on leap-year day (Feb 29th) for good luck. If she should be refused, her suitor is required to pay her a 'fine': enough fabric to make a skirt.

"Chains do not hold a marriage together. It is thread, hundreds of tiny threads, which sew people together through the years."

SIMONE SIGNORET

Tying the knot

When two people come together, whether in traditional marriage or to forge a sacred union, they make a lifetime connection. The creation of this bond is often referred to as 'tying the knot,' and while this fits symbolically, there are also other connotations, with roots in ancient times.

The Romans fitted young brides with a girdle comprised of several strong knots. The groom had to undo them before the marriage could be consummated. Some scholars believe this is where the famous phrase originated; the knots of chastity were undone, so that husband and wife could come together and form a new bond.

The Celts had their own version of tying the knot with a simple handfasting ceremony. The couple's hands were entwined, and they would 'jump the broom' together: a practice associated with sweeping away the past and looking to the future as a couple.

Another theory relates to a seafaring practice, whereby loved-up sailors would send their sweethearts a length of rope to indicate their intentions to marry. If one of the ladies in question felt the same, she tied a knot in it before sending it back.

"*Marriage is the proper remedy. It is the most natural state of man, and therefore the state in which you are most likely to find solid happiness.*"

BENJAMIN FRANKLIN
Advice to a Young Man on the Choice of a Mistress (1745)

Wedding customs

Love may be universal, but you can say 'I do' in many different ways, depending on where you live. From quirky to crazy, these traditions are considered an essential part of the wedding ceremony, and just another way to secure your 'happy ever after'.

Don't break into a smile if you choose the Congo as a place to get hitched. Brides and grooms must not reveal their true joy. A solemn face is required throughout the entire ceremony, as this shows that the couple are serious about the impending nuptials.

In Fiji, it's tradition for the prospective groom to offer the bride's father a whale's tooth when asking for her hand in marriage. Failure to do so could result in no wedding.

Chinese grooms like to play cupid. They are encouraged to shoot their brides several times with a bow and arrow (*sans* arrowheads). The arrows are then collected and broken during the ceremony to cement their love.

A well-fed wife is key to wealth and happiness in Mauritius. The bride-to-be is encouraged to pile on the pounds before the wedding.

In Greece, the best man must add shaving the groom to his list of duties on the wedding day. Once buffed and suited, the groom will then be fed honey and almonds by his new mother-in-law.

In France, newlyweds consume huge amounts of chocolate and Champagne – from a chamber pot!

German couples are set to work tidying up broken porcelain, which are smashed at their feet by the wedding guests. The idea is that this will help to instil a sense of teamwork into their marriage.

Traditional Shinto wedding ceremonies are formal affairs. The bride wears white from head to toe, including a giant hood, called a *suno kakushi*, which is thought to hide her twin 'horns of jealousy' – ego and selfishness – from her prospective in-laws.

'Blackening the bride' is a popular Scottish custom. The day before the wedding, the bride (and sometimes the groom) is kidnapped by her loved ones and smeared with fish, treacle and rotten eggs. Once covered from head to toe, she is paraded through the streets, an ancient tradition which is said to prepare her for the trials and tribulations of married life.

The Masai tribe of Kenya don't like to tempt fate by showing too much support for their newlyweds. Instead, the bride's father spits on her as she leaves the party with her new husband.

Russian newlyweds share a giant sweetbread known as a *karavaya*. Interlaced with rings, to represent a faithful union, and wheat (for prosperity), it's thought that whoever takes the biggest bite without using their hands will be the head of the family!

" There is nothing nobler or more admirable than when two people who see eye to eye keep house as man and wife, confounding their enemies and delighting their friends."

HOMER
The Odyssey, Book VI

" *It is not lack of love but lack of friendship that makes unhappy marriages.* "

NIETZSCHE

While most customs are fun and based on folklore, it is possible to create a ritual that is unique to you as a couple and embodies the values you hold dear. Whether you follow a traditional route, or prefer to take inspiration from ancient practices, give the ceremony a personal twist.

Start by considering what is important to you both: your shared beliefs, qualities and interests. For example, there might be a book that means a great deal to both of you, or a picture of somewhere you've visited as a couple. Perhaps you each have something different that you'd like to bring together to commemorate your union.

Next, find a way of including these things in the ceremony – you might read some words from the book or have the picture present while you make your commitment. This ritual is unique to you as a couple, and something you can draw strength from. It should be something that you can repeat at any time in the future without expensive frills, as a way of reconnecting and cementing your bond.

Find your 'Us'

As weddings celebrate the love of two
people, it's natural that romance is in
the air. Folklore is littered with tips
on how to find your soulmate at such
occasions. According to one old wives'
tale, single ladies in attendance should
slip a piece of wedding cake beneath
their pillow at night if they want to
dream of a future husband. Another
suggests that should the youngest
sister marry first, the older sibling
must dance barefoot all night long
to ensure she finds a match.

"In this a journey is like marriage. The certain way to be wrong is to think you control it."

JOHN STEINBECK
*Travels with Charley:
In Search of America*

Honeymoon

During the fifth century, time was measured in lunar cycles in most European cultures, and the ancients looked to the skies to mark important events. When a couple wed, it was tradition to provide them with a 'moon' of mead, which translates as roughly a month's worth of sweet wine made from fermented honey. The couple were encouraged to share this together in a bid to consummate the marriage and quickly conceive, thus ensuring the continuation of the bloodline. Most scholars believe this is where the term 'honeymoon' comes from.

"...for our honeymoon will shine our life long: its beams will only fade over your grave or mine."

CHARLOTTE BRONTË
Jane Eyre

"Wherever you go, go with all your heart."

CONFUCIUS

Couples wanting to save money but still spend quality time together, post-wedding, often opt for a 'mini moon'. The principle is the same, but the holiday only lasts for a couple of days and is usually a city break.

" Travel is like love, mostly because it's a heightened state of awareness in which we are mindful, receptive, undimmed by familiarity and ready to be transformed. That is why the best trips, like the best love affairs, never really end."

PICO IYER

"I loved her against reason, against promise, against peace, against hope, against happiness, against all discouragement that could be."

CHARLES DICKENS
Great Expectations

"Never go on trips with anyone you do not love."

ERNEST HEMINGWAY

"Each blade of grass has its spot on earth whence it draws its life, its strength; and so is man rooted to the land from which he draws his faith together with his life."

JOSEPH CONRAD
Lord Jim

The landscape, and all that makes up our environment, is key to constructing the identity of us as a planet.

You might already have your 'us'; you might be searching for it. You might be cultivating it like a flower, watching as the relationship blooms. The truth is, without the earth beneath your feet and the sky above your head, there would be no 'us'. It – and you – would cease to exist.

"And while I stood there I saw more than I can tell and I understood more than I saw; for I was seeing in a sacred manner the shapes of all things in the spirit, and the shape of all shapes as they must live together like one being."

NICHOLAS BLACK ELK
*Black Elk Speaks: Being the Life
Story of a Holy Man of the Oglala Sioux*

When we understand the nature of the world, and how everything is connected, we come to appreciate the emotional connections in our own life.

"Look deep into nature, and then you will understand everything better."

ALBERT EINSTEIN

Walk together in nature and marvel at its beauty. Breathe in the peace, and let the vista renew your hopes and dreams. Recognise the power of love, from the tiniest flower bud, bathed in the warmth of the sun, to the tallest tree, and how it shades all those that gather close. Care for each other in the same way, with tender affection and continued strength.

Nurture the land together, and watch your relationship grow in new and exciting ways.

"*The garden of love is green without limit and yields many fruits other than sorrow or joy. Love is beyond either condition; without spring, without autumn, it is always fresh.*"

RUMI

Appreciate the great outdoors. Go for long walks in companionable silence. Take in your surroundings and engage all of your senses, then be sure to share the things you've seen.

Create a space for 'us' outside, depending on the room you have. Come up with a list of plants and flowers you'd like to grow and how you'd like the space to work. Formulate a plan where you share the gardening duties, but also be sure to spend time together, planting and tending the area. Most importantly, enjoy the garden you're building together.

Grow your own vegetables and herbs and use them to cook tasty and nourishing meals together. The experience of eating a meal is enhanced when we know where the food on the table comes from.

Extend your 'us' to include wildlife and other animals. Get to know the birds in your garden and make a point of feeding them. Look out for other signs of life – smaller mammals and insects – and consider how you can make them feel at home. For example, you might want to build a bug hotel or invest in a bee box. Make your garden accessible and safe for creatures like hedgehogs.

Get on top of your recycling and
make an action plan together to be
energy efficient, and re-use as much
as possible.

Explore your local countryside and try and visit somewhere new at least once a month. Get a map and pinpoint areas of interest and things you'd like to do and see. Get out into the world together.

"Conservation is a state of harmony between men and land."

ALDO LEOPOLD

To Be Us

To be us is to be united.

A twosome, a pair.

Not always together,

but always there.

Wherever we wander

our hearts side by side,

We two are a couple,

partners, a tribe.

With the sun on our back

and the earth at our feet,

A smile on each face

There is something unspoken;
We don't need to say.
We know we are 'us'
Every moment, each day.

Til death us do part

In the animal kingdom there are certain species of animals that will remain faithful until separated by death.

Lar gibbons are one of the only primates that practise monogamy. They can live for 35 to 40 years and during their lifetime they will form strong bonds with their partner, grooming each other and hanging out in the trees. They also exhibit a surprising amount of gender equality throughout their relationship, especially when it comes to raising their family as they share the care of their young.

Long-distance relationships aren't easy, but bald eagles thrive in them. The birds fly solo during the winter and migration, reconnecting with their mates each breeding season. Most eagles pair by the age of five and stay together for at least 20 years.

Only about three per cent of mammals are exclusive. Beavers show us how it is done, as after mating, they will spend as much time maintaining their relationships as they do their dams. The males and females co-parent their young and stay together until one partner in the pairing dies.

Mute swans are a true symbol of love. A pairing will return to the same nest year after year and the male swan will go out of his way to prove his commitment by helping his female mate to build the nest, protecting his family from potential threats and sharing egg incubation duties.

Barn owls put all their eggs in one basket and use their own language of love. The males woo the ladies with screeches and gifts of dead mice. If the female then responds with crocking sounds, she's basically saying, "I do".

Let's treasure and cherish the time spent together, the memories we continue to make. One day it might not just be us, but another two-letter word: we, our family. So let's always remember the roots of who we are and how it started – with 'us'.

"My heart to you is given:
Oh, do give yours to me;
We'll lock them up together,
And throw away the key."

ARTHUR FREDERICK SAUNDERS

Down on one knee

There is a lot of speculation as to how this gesture, technically known as genuflection, came about.

In the Middle Ages, during the days of chivalry and knighthood, men would typically go down on one knee before the women they adored. Medieval knights would also kneel before their lords in the ultimate sign of loyalty and obedience and on the battlefield, kneeling would signal the act of surrendering or begging for mercy.

Bending down on one knee has come to symbolise the man's humble acknowledgement that, by marrying his beloved, he is choosing to leave behind his days as a bachelor, and fully commit to the desires and needs of his future spouse. Kneeling also demonstrates the inherent trust between partners, as well as the man's devotion for bringing their two lives together. The intimacy of this special moment is heightened as the man uses his vulnerable physical position to demonstrate the deep emotional connection between himself and his beloved. Cute!

Wedding shoes

This wedding tradition is believed to have stemmed from the Ancient Egyptian custom of swapping sandals after the exchange of goods. The bride's father would give his daughter's shoes to the groom to symbolise that she is now his property, and consequently no longer the responsibility of her father.

This tradition could have also originated from a fifth-century custom, that carried on well into the Tudor period. As the wedding carriage drove away with the happy couple, it was traditional for guests to throw their shoes. Hitting the departing vehicle was seen as good luck, and a sign of fertility. Today, we have realised how dangerous this is – plus what a waste of shoes! – so instead footwear is tied to the bumper of the getaway car. The knots themselves are symbolic of how the newly married couple are 'tied' together in their commitment to one another.

Over the threshold

In ancient times, it was believed that the bride was vulnerable to evil spirits, particularly through the soles of her feet. Evil spirits supposedly hung out on the threshold of homes, thus the bride was carried over by her man to protect her from anything that could already be lurking in the couple's new home.

Some Europeans believed that if the bride tripped on her way into the new house, it would bring bad luck to both her marriage and her home. The risk of falling is eliminated when the groom carries in his beautiful new bride.

Queen Victoria started the Western world's white wedding dress trend in 1840 – before then, brides simply wore their best dress.

Famous as an 'Us'

Often in history, bonds between two people are so strong that the individual identity fades and the partners become remembered as a pair. From the earliest of creation stories in the Garden of Eden to the most endearing of cartoon characters, two, are stronger than one.

How strange to imagine an owl without a pussycat or a Rogers without an Astaire or, heaven forbid, a Harry without a Meghan.

Famous pairs

Adam and Eve

Samson and Delilah

Anthony and Cleopatra

Lancelot and Guinevere

Romeo and Juliet

Tarzan and Jane

Simone de Beauvoir and
Jean-Paul Sartre

Bonnie and Clyde

John and Jackie Kennedy

Lady and the Tramp

Will and Kate

'It's us against the world' – so the old saying goes. There is a deep wisdom to the idea that a couple, with a strong foundation, can take on whatever life throws at them. As part of an 'Us' there is always someone to talk to, someone to confide in, someone to share dreams with and someone to create beauty with. In turn, the small team of two can go out into the world and shape it for the better.

" The strength of a nation derives from the integrity of the home. "

CONFUCIUS

The brilliance of 'Us'

Working in partnership, as an 'Us', can help to achieve more than slogging away alone. Not necessarily romantically entwined, working with someone on a shared passion more than doubles your chances of success.

Be inspired by the scientific and creative partnerships celebrated here. Just think of Warner Bros, Rogers and Hammerstein, Hewlett Packard, Ben & Jerry's, Proctor & Gamble...

James Watson and Francis Crick – discovered the structure of DNA.

Andrew Lloyd Webber and Tim Rice – composer and lyricist, Lloyd Webber and Rice have worked together on creating some of the world's best musicals including *Jesus Christ Superstar* and *Evita*.

Marie and Pierre Curie – husband and wife were scientific collaborators who studied radiation and discovered elements of radium and polonium.

Frida Kahlo and Diego Rivera – Mexican artists whose stormy marriage inspired fantastic paintings.

Ismail Merchant and James Ivory – lovers, business partners and makers of films including *Room with a View* and *Howard's End*.

Being part of an 'Us', whether in love, in friendship, or in business, means that you will never stop growing. One part of the 'Us' gives to the other, the other takes, and then the taker gives and the giver takes.

From small smiles, laughs and jokes, to deep understanding, honour and ideas, being part of an 'Us' becomes a life long partnership with sharing at its heart.

"Friendship is essentially a partnership."

ARISTOTLE

If you are feeling alone, outside of an 'Us' remember the red thread. Be proactive in finding the friend, the lover, the partner, who completes you. Feel for the thread and search.

Smile and open conversations with people you meet on a daily basis, the man in the shop, the woman at the coffee bar, the commuter on the train. Ask yourself what is lacking, pick up the thread and follow it to new clubs, new courses, new beginnings. If there are people from your life that you miss, pick up the thread and get back in touch. You are already part of an 'Us', pick up the thread and find it.

"No man is an island."

JOHN DONNE

Married couples are buried in the same plot, doomed lovers are reunited on the other side, and descendants physically demonstrate how, once united, a couple, never truly separates. Their unity always lives on, either in memorials, in children, or in the memories of those who knew them. The idea of the red thread binding soulmates together does not end after death, it just comes full circle.

"It is perfectly certain that the soul is immortal and imperishable, and our souls will actually exist in another world."

SOCRATES

"People who need people are the luckiest people in the world."

BOB MERRILL

In this age of strident individualism, where apparent worth is given by how many likes you receive, how many followers you have and how well you are able to package yourself to the world, there is a fear that perhaps relying on someone else is a sign of weakness.

This is tosh. Humans are created to love and to join with another. Finding someone to share your journey with does not mean a dilution of the self – it is the very opposite – the strengthening of the self and the strengthening of another.

Close the door. Shut the window. Put down your phone.

Let no-one else in. Part of the sheer joy of being part of an 'Us' is indulging in each other together. Alone with each other. Make time to savour each other's company alone without intrusions, without others, without distractions. Keep a time of the week sacred for 'Us' time and wallow in what you most love about each other.

**Make time this week to enjoy
all of the below, together:**

Laugh

Cook

Dance

Eat

Play

Kiss

Walk

Rest

Bathe

Sleep

Creating a closed world of 'Us' does not happen immediately, rather it evolves over time as life is experienced together, memories are made and challenges overcome. Sometimes traditions creep up on you, without you realising, and before you know it, a ritual of your unique partnership has been created. Whatever the rituals are, whether small and ordinary to extravagant and lavish, note them down in a treasury because the details are unique to you both.

Our rituals:

At Christmas we love to…

For birthdays we love to…

Our favourite morning is…

Our favourite meal is…

We relax together by…

When we hear this music we…

In spring we enjoy…

We spend our holidays…

The first thing we do in the morning is…

The last thing we do at night is…

There is one partnership, above all others that seriously put the 'Us' into the USA. Second President John Adams and his wife Abigail shared a 50-year marriage, a political alliance and created a dynasty that shaped a whole country. Between them, they witnessed revolution, war, separation and the birth of the independent American nation. Often apart they maintained their bond by writing frequently. Over 1,000 of their letters are preserved and tell a story of exhilarating union – of minds, love and country.

*"More than kisses,
letters mingle souls."*

JOHN DONNE

While of course being part of an 'Us' does not diminish your individuality, it is mindful and wise to work with your other half to create a harmonious whole. Form good habits together, follow each other's rhythms and seek to exist in unison.

Where there are areas of friction, work together to make smooth. Are you a night owl, your other half a morning lark? Do you enjoy different food?

There is never any need to feel annoyed. Instead, work out ways to meet in the middle, alternate, take turns and seek to turn your differences into a united whole.

"Let us be grateful to people who make us happy, they are the charming gardeners who make our souls blossom."

MARCEL PROUST

BIBLIOGRAPHY

Brontë, Charlotte., *Jane Eyre* (1847)

Conrad, Joseph., *Lord Jim* (1899)

Gibran, Khalil., *The Prophet* (1923)

Hawthorne, Nathaniel., *The American Notebooks* (1840)

Hesse, Herman., *Narziß und Goldmund* (1930)

Hugo, Victor., *Les Misérables* (1862)

Raymond, John G. Neihardt, *Black Elk Speaks: Being the life Story of a Holy Man of the Oglala Sioux* (1932)

Steinbeck, John., *Travels with Charley: In Search of America* (1962)

Stevenson, Robert Louis., *Virginibus Puerisque* (1881)

FURTHER READING

Austen, Jane., *Pride and Prejudice* (1813)

Rowan, Tiddy., *The Little Book of Love* (Quadrille, 2015)

Shakespeare, William., *Romeo and Juliet* (1597)

FILMS

As Dixon Steele in a Lonely Place, directed by Nicholas Ray (Sony Pictures Home Entertainment, 1950)

The Notebook, directed by Nick Cassavetes (New Line Cinema, 2004)

When Harry met Sally, directed by Rob Reiner (Castle Rock Entertainment, 1989)

QUOTES ARE TAKEN FROM

Abigail Adams: Wife of John Adams, the second President of the USA.

Albert Einstein was a theoretical physicist. He is renowned for developing the general theory of relativity and recieved the Nobel Prize for Physcis in 1921.

Louisa May Alcott: 19th century American novelist, author of *Little Women*.

Viv Apple: 21st century English poet.

Aristotle: Ancient Greek philosopher and scientist.

Nicholas Black Elk: A holy man of the Oglala Sioux who converted to Catholicism.

Humphrey Bogart: American film star and stage actor.

Charlotte Brontë: 19th century English writer, author of *Jane Eyre*.

Rupert Brooke: 20th century poet who wrote *The Solider*.

Pierre Teilhard De Chardin: French idealist philosopher.

Confucius: Chinese sage who lived in the 6th century BC.

Joseph Conrad: Polish / British writer who wrote *Heart of Darkness*.

Marlene Dietrich: German actress and singer.

John Donne: 17th century metaphysical poet.

Benjamin Franklin: American polymath and one of the Founding Fathers.

Robert Frost: 20th century American poet.

Khalil Gibran: American / Lebanese writer and author of *The Prophet*.

Nathaniel Hawthorne: 19th century American writer, author of *The Scarlet Letter*.

Ernest Hemingway: 20th century writer, author of *The Old Man and the Sea*.

Jimi Hendrix: American rock guitarist and singer song writer.

Hermann Hesse: German born novelist, poet and painter.

Homer: Legendary Ancient Greek author of *The Iliad* and *The Odyssey*.

Victor Hugo: 19th century French writer, author of *Les Misérables*.

Pico Iyer: Essayist and novelist.

Helen Keller: Deaf, blind American author, political activist and lecturer.

Jiddu Krishnamurti: 20th century Indian philosopher.

Henry Wadsworth Longfellow: American poet who wrote *The Song of Hiawatha*.

John Lennon: Beatle, 20th century legend.

Aldo Leopold: US author and conservationist.

Martin Luther: 16th century German monk.

Bob Merrill: American songwriter.

Fr Thomas Merton: Trappist monk.

Mother Teresa: Catholic nun and missionary.

Nietzsche: 19th century German philosopher.

Marcel Proust: French novelist who wrote *Remembrance of Things Past.*

Rumi: 13th century Persian poet.

Antoine De Saint-Exupéry: French writer.

Ryunosuke Satoro: Japanese writer.

Arthur Frederick Saunders: English recipient of the Victoria Cross.

Simone Signoret: French cinema actress.

Socrates: Ancient Greek founder of Western philosophy.

Gertrude Stein: American novelist and playwright.

John Steinbeck: American author who wrote, *Of Mice and Men.*

Robert Louis Stevenson: Scottish novelist who wrote *Treasure Island.*

Walt Whitman: An American humanist and writer.

Oscar Wilde: 19th century English writer and wit, author of *Dorian Gray.*

William Butler Yeats: was an Irish poet and leading literary figure of the 20th century.

Publishing Director Sarah Lavelle
Editor Harriet Butt
Editorial Assistant Harriet Webster
Words Alison Davies, Joanna Gray
Series Designer Emily Lapworth
Designer Monika Adamczyk
Production Director Vincent Smith
Production Controller Sinead Hering

Published in 2019 by Quadrille,
an imprint of Hardie Grant Publishing

Quadrille
52-54 Southwark Street
London SE1 1UN
quadrille.com

Cataloguing in Publication Data: a catalogue record for
this book is available from the British Library.

ISBN 978 1 78713 378 5

Printed in China